Tunes That Teach
Spelling

12 Lively Tunes and Hands-On Activities That Teach Spelling Rules, Patterns, and Tricky Words

by Marcia Miller
with Martin Lee

NEW YORK • TORONTO • LONDON • AUCKLAND • SYDNEY
MEXICO CITY • NEW DELHI • HONG KONG • BUENOS AIRES

Teaching Resources

Dedication

To **Schenectady**, my hometown
and the first really long, hard word I learned to spell—
and to everyone there who encouraged my musical interests
—M.M.

Credits

Lyrics: Marcia Miller
Music: Jeff Waxman
Lead Vocals: Marcia Miller
Backup Vocals: Lisa Asher, Bryan Johnson, Martin Lee, Marcia Miller
Produced and arranged by Jeff Waxman at Waxtrax Recording, New York, NY

Cover design by Maria Lilja
Cover illustrations by Debbie Palen
Interior design by Jeffrey Dorman
Interior illustrations by Mike Moran

Book ISBN 0-439-32317-7
Product ISBN 0-439-32069-0
Copyright © 2005 by Marcia Miller and Martin Lee
All rights reserved.
Printed in the U.S.A.

3 4 5 6 7 8 9 10   40   12 11 10 09 08 07

CONTENTS

Dear Teacher,

As you undoubtedly have observed in your own class, most children are natural-born musicians who respond easily and freely to melody, rhythm, and rhyme. Memorization rarely feels like a chore to students when they learn by associating what they need to know with the words, rhythms, cadences, or sound effects of a song.

This is exactly why we have created *Tunes That Teach Spelling*. The CD in this book offers 12 original songs in different musical styles with varying lyrical content. Learning and singing the songs can help students become better spellers of written English.

Each song in this album focuses on a particular spelling rule, pattern, anomaly, or "spelling demon." Each song stands alone; together, the set provides a musical link to an important piece of your language arts curriculum.

The songs of *Tunes That Teach Spelling* approach spelling in various ways. They

- ♫ present a rule for students to memorize and apply with regularity;
- ♫ offer examples of spelling "traps";
- ♫ compare and contrast similar words that tend to cause spelling problems;
- ♫ highlight notable letters or sounds;
- ♫ sort and classify words by recognizable patterns;
- ♫ explore ways to learn long words.

We hope that you and your students will enjoy approaching spelling in this way.

Harmoniously yours,

Marcia Miller

How to Use This Book and CD

Naturally, you are the best judge of how to incorporate *Tunes That Teach Spelling* into your language arts program or into any particular lesson plan. Regardless of your own musical background, tastes, or experiences, you'll appreciate how quickly most students will embrace these songs as enjoyable learning devices. The steady rhythms, tuneful melodies, and catchy rhymes of *Tunes That Teach Spelling* are sure to lead to a classroom of clapping hands, bobbing heads, shaking shoulders, and tapping toes.

Here are some suggestions for using this book and CD:

♫ Play the songs regularly to help students learn the lyrics, which will, in turn, help improve their spelling skills. Consider these times for playing all or part of the *Tunes That Teach Spelling* CD:
- as kids enter the classroom in the morning
- as they get ready to begin language arts
- as they line up for lunch, recess, or dismissal
- as background music during free time
- anytime, just for fun!

♫ Photocopy the lyrics pages so students can have their own copies. Keep a full set of lyrics in a special spelling folder, or laminate each page for durability.

♫ Prepare students for any unfamiliar words or expressions in the lyrics that might puzzle them, such as "go scot-free" in "Contractions."

♫ Point out particular literary devices used in the lyrics to extend students' learning into other areas of language arts. For example, "Why Change *Y* to *I*?" includes several similes, such as "...dandy as a honeybee..." You might have students write their own similes to help them describe the stumbling blocks in certain difficult words.

♫ Set up a *Tunes That Teach Spelling* listening center in your classroom. Provide the CD, a CD player (or computer with a CD player in it), headphones, and junction boxes; include the song sheets so students can follow along as they listen.

♫ Have a "Speller's Choice" time, when students can request to hear and sing their favorite song.

♫ Encourage the musical/rhythmic learners in your class to make up their own original spelling songs, chants, raps, or tunes they can share with classmates. Or, invite them to make up new verses to the existing songs.

♫ Help students create displays, dioramas, or murals relating to the different songs. For example, to extend the ideas in "Silent *E*," students could list math words that end with silent *e*, such as *nine*, *square*, *divide*, or *whole*.

SPELLING ACE

GOAL: To help students learn to spell some common long words

KEY CONCEPTS/RULES

There are no particular rules to apply to learn to spell long words. But there are many effective techniques that can help in the process:

- Break down the words into smaller parts.
- Identify prefixes, suffixes, base words, or familiar word roots.
- Think about known spelling patterns and rules from simpler words.
- Focus on any tricky part of the word to avoid misspelling it.

RELATED WORDS

administration	independence	responsibility
autobiography	kindergarten	temperature
California	marshmallow	transformation
disadvantage	misunderstanding	unconventional
entertainment	Pennsylvania	underestimate
geographical	pronunciation	unsatisfactory
hippopotamus	representative	

ACTIVITY IDEAS

1 Set up an interactive word wall. Divide it into sections according to the number of syllables or number of letters in long words. Invite students to add examples to the proper section of the word wall of any long words they encounter while reading, speaking, or listening. Choose several of these words to be part of your weekly spelling list.

2 Challenge musical and rhythmic learners to use some of the long words to create additional verses for this song. Or, invite them to create their own rhythmic chants that can help them learn to spell challenging long words.

3 Work with students to create an alphabetical gazetteer of place names that contain ten letters or more. You might wish to restrict this collection to place names within your own state, anywhere in America, or around the world, depending on the geographical sophistication of your students.

WALTZING ENDINGS

GOAL: To reinforce the meaning of the suffix *-ble* (capable of or fit for), and to provide examples of its variant spellings: *-able* and *-ible*

KEY CONCEPTS/RULES

• Unfortunately, there is no hard-and-fast rule to determine whether the suffix *-ble* is spelled *-able* or *-ible*. In general, more English words take the *-able* spelling than the *-ible*. As is the case with many English spelling anomalies, the most accurate method is to become familiar with the words that use this ending and consult a dictionary to be sure.

• Consider the rules for soft *c* and soft *g* to determine how to spell this suffix. (See "Soft *C*, Soft *G*," page 15.) In general, use *-ible* for base words or word roots that end in soft *c* or soft *g* (e.g., *tangible, forcible*).

RELATED WORDS

acceptable	irritable	collectible	incredible
agreeable	memorable	convertible	plausible
breakable	questionable	divisible	reproducible
comfortable	regrettable	edible	responsible
disposable	unbelievable	horrible	sensible
flammable	valuable	illegible	visible

ACTIVITY IDEAS

1 Provide a list of assorted base words. Give each pair of students index cards with *-able* and *-ible* printed on them. Have students form new words by adding the proper suffix to the given base words. Model how to use the index cards to "test" the endings, to see which one looks right to the eye. Encourage students to consult a dictionary to confirm the correct spelling.

2 Challenge students to create additional verses for the song.

K-N

GOAL: To familiarize students with numerous words that begin with silent *k*

KEY CONCEPTS/RULES

- In English, *k* is usually silent when it precedes *n* to begin a word or a syllable (e.g., *knock, knife, doorknob*).
- There is no trick to mastering this spelling irregularity. The most reliable approach is to become familiar with the words that begin with *kn* to know to include the silent *k*.

NOTE: Be sure students recognize that in this song, the silent *k* in each word that includes *kn* has been intentionally (and incorrectly!) pronounced for humorous effect.

RELATED WORDS

knack	kneel	knight	knot
knapsack	knell	knit	knowledge
knave	knickers	knob	known
knead	knickknack	knock	knuckle
knee	knife	knoll	knurl

ACTIVITY IDEAS

1 Provide students with sentences and/or paragraphs that include words and/or syllables that begin with the /n/ sound spelled the regular way and with *kn*. Change all the words so they are spelled with *kn*. Challenge students to proofread and correct the words, as necessary. Here is an example:

> Richard Knixon was the 37th President of the Uknited States. He served in the Knavy during World War II. Knixon won the Republican knomination for president in 1960, but did knot win that election.

2 A similar spelling anomaly is the use of silent *g* before *n*, as in *gnarl, gnash, gnat, gnaw,* and *gnome*. Invite students to browse through a dictionary for examples of *gn* words. Challenge them to create silly poems like the verses of this song, but that feature *gn* words.

SILENT *E*

GOAL: To reinforce and model how silent *e* affects vowel sound

KEY CONCEPTS/RULES

- When the letter *e* follows a vowel and a consonant (VCe), this pattern usually indicates that the vowel makes a long sound. Variants of this pattern include VCe (*ace*), CVCe (*lace*), and CCVCe (*place*).
- Final *e* (also known as silent *e* or *e*-marker) controls many sound distinctions in words such as *pat/pate, flak/flake, grip/gripe, and mod/mode*.
- Silent *e* often signals that a preceding *g* or *c* is soft, as in *rage* or *price*.
- English words rarely end in *v*. Silent *e* in words such as *love, give*, and *prove* therefore violates the long-vowel rule in favor of orthographic consistency.

RELATED WORDS

bit/bite	hid/hide	past/paste	shin/shine
cap/cape	human/humane	prim/prime	slim/slime
dim/dime	lam/lame	rob/robe	strip/stripe
fad/fade	not/note	sag/sage	unit/unite
gal/gale	pal/pale	scrap/scrape	van/vane
glad/glade	pan/pane	sham/shame	wad/wade

ACTIVITY IDEAS

1 Write words with short vowel/long vowel contrasts on sets of index cards (see Related Words above). Shuffle the cards, deal them out randomly, and have each student locate the person who holds the related card. Extend by challenging the pairs to create two related sentences, each using one of the words. For example: *The light in the room was* dim. *I couldn't find the* dime *I dropped*.

2 Provide students with two- and three-syllable words that end with a silent *e* phonogram, such as *alcove, alpine, anecdote, canine, capsize, dynamite, electrode, estate, hesitate, lubricate, marmalade, pigeonhole, propose, provoke, sacrifice, satellite, saxophone, senile, stargaze, stethoscope, subside, televise, transcribe, upgrade, wardrobe, worthwhile*. Have students pronounce the word and indicate the long vowel controlled by the final *e*. Then have them use a dictionary to determine the meaning of the word so that they can use it in a sentence.

DOUBLE TROUBLE

GOAL: To reinforce the rule that double consonants usually signal a short vowel sound; to highlight pairs of words that differ in spelling only in having a single or double consonant

KEY CONCEPTS/RULES

- Double the final consonant before adding a suffix if the word
  - ✔ has one syllable, or the final syllable is accented (*bob + ed = bobbed; befit + ing = befitting*)
  - ✔ ends in a single consonant, except *x* (*beg + ing = begging; tax + ed = taxed*)
  - ✔ has a single vowel letter (*ram + ing = ramming; nap + ed = napped*)
- Double the final consonant before adding a suffix if the suffix begins with a vowel (*rub + ing = rubbing*)
- Double the final consonant before adding a suffix if the word has two syllables and is accented on the last syllable (*admit + ance = admittance*)
- Do NOT double the final consonant if
  - ✔ the suffix begins with a consonant (*cup + ful = cupful*)
  - ✔ the vowel is a digraph (has two letters) (*moan + ed = moaned*)
  - ✔ the word has two final consonants (*chart + ing = charting*)
  - ✔ the final syllable is unaccented (*benefit + ed = benefited; equal + ing = equaling*)

RELATED WORDS

capped/caped	hatter/hater	mopping/moping
fatted/fated	hopped/hoped	robbing/robing
filled/filed	latter/later	snipped/sniped
gapped/gaped	manned/maned	tilling/tiling

ACTIVITY IDEAS

1 Challenge students to make up additional verses for the song. Invite those who wish to perform to sing their verses for the class.

2 Present groups of nonsense words that follow the rules of doubling as exemplified in the song. Examples include: *plobbing/plobing, fritting/friting, dapping/daping, tumming/ tuming, zlipping/zliping.* Have students apply the rules to pronounce the words correctly. Encourage them to make up their own words.

3 Dictate several sentences or phrases that include related words. Encourage students to think about the vowel sound they hear to help them spell the words correctly.

WHY CHANGE Y TO I?

GOAL: To highlight the need to change final *y* to *i* before adding certain suffixes or inflected endings

KEY CONCEPTS/RULES

In words that end with *y*, notice which letter precedes the *y*:

• If it is a consonant, change the *y* to *i* before adding a suffix or ending. (*sturdy + er = sturdier; easy + est = easiest*)

• If it is a vowel, do NOT change the *y* to *i*. (*toy + ing = toying; play + ed = played*)

RELATED WORDS

army	hazy	rally	sneaky
bury	heavy	ready	study
carry	hurry	sandy	trophy
deny	lobby	sassy	vary
ferry	marry	saucy	wacky
flaky	pony	shady	zany

ACTIVITY IDEAS

1 Provide students with an assortment of words that end with *y* preceded by a consonant (see Related Words above) and a list of common suffixes or inflected endings that could be combined with those words. Encourage students to form new words by changing the *y* to *i* and adding the ending. Invite volunteers to use their words in sentences.

2 Provide a list of words in which the final *y* does not change when an ending is added. Examples include *joy, stay, pray, annoy, betray, key*. Guide students to notice the difference in endings added to these examples.

HOMOPHONES

GOAL: To define homophones and to provide mnemonics that help students correctly distinguish and spell pairs of homophones

KEY CONCEPTS/RULES

• The terms *homophone* and *homonym* are often used interchangeably. Definitions vary, but homophones always have different spellings; some sources include *homographs* with homonyms. Homographs are words that have the same spelling but different meanings (such as *mouse*, the rodent, and *mouse*, the computer accessory).

• The popularity and availability of spell-checking software makes it especially important for today's writers to recognize homophones. This is because most software will not flag the incorrect usage of a homophone as long as it sees a correctly spelled word—even one that has been misused!

RELATED WORDS

aisle/isle	capital/capitol	loan/lone	plain/plane
allowed/aloud	ceiling/sealing	loot/lute	pole/poll
bail/bale	die/dye	maize/maze	profit/prophet
bare/bear	flour/flower	medal/meddle	ring/wring
bazaar/bizarre	hoarse/horse	muscle/mussel	slay/sleigh

ACTIVITY IDEAS

1 Here's a bonus verse (the song would've been too long had we included it!):

> The job of any *principal* is to run the public school.
> But the other *principle*, you know, is a belief or it is a rule.
> P-R-I-N-C-I-, they start, but how do these homophones end?
> P-L-E for the rule or law, P-A-L for the friend.

Invite students to sing this verse together.

2 Assign each student a pair of homophones. Challenge students to determine the meaning for each word, and then use it in a sentence that demonstrates its meaning. Encourage them to think of mnemonics to help them remember which word is which. Invite small groups of students to have homophone "teach-ins," where they take turns instructing one another about the homophones they have learned.

3 Set up a simple bulletin board display called "Highlighting Homophones." Each day or so, post a new pair of homophones. Invite students to use both words in daily conversation.

SNEAKY O-U-G-H

GOAL: To highlight the *o-u-g-h* combination, which can represent six different sounds

KEY CONCEPTS/RULES

The letter combination *-ough* appears in many English words. Learning to spell this combination is not so problematic. The true difficulty comes in trying to determine which of the six distinct sounds these letters make.

RELATED WORDS

cough	although	brought	bough
enough	borough	fought	drought
rough	doughnut	ought	plough
slough	furlough	sought	
tough	sourdough	thought	through
trough	thorough	wrought	

ACTIVITY IDEAS

1 Guide students to analyze the organization of the verses in this song. Help them recognize that each verse focuses on one particular sound made by *-ough*. Challenge students to find other words spelled with *-ough* that make the same sound as the examples given in each verse.

2 Create a deck of assorted *-ough* words on separate index cards. Challenge students to sort the words by the particular sound the *-ough* makes.

TRICKY SILENT LETTERS

GOAL: To help students correctly spell common words that have a silent letter

KEY CONCEPTS/RULES

- Most of the letters in the English alphabet are silent at one time or another. One reason for this is that English has borrowed many words from other languages—along with unexpected spelling patterns. Another reason is that some English words are spelled according to archaic rules. Also, pronunciation may have changed over time, while the spelling has stayed the same.

- Common silent letters found in English include the *t* in *tch* (*hitch*), the *d* in *dg* (*badge*), the *w* in *wr* (*write*), the *k* in *kn* (*knot*), the *g* in *gn* (*gnome*), the *b* in *mb* (*lamb*), the *p* in *ps* (*psychic*), the *l* in *lk* or *lm* (*walk, calm*), the *h* in *rh* (*rhino*).

- There are no particular rules to apply to learn to spell words with unexpected spellings. The best tactic may be to learn to recognize such words and identify the spelling irregularity in each.

RELATED WORDS

adjective	exhausted	match	shepherd
autumn	fasten	palm	soften
ballet	gnaw	phlegm	thumb
climb	handkerchief	pterodactyl	would
column	honesty	rhubarb	wrestle
daughter	island	rhythm	wrist
excellent	khaki	science	yacht

ACTIVITY IDEAS

1 Provide lists of words that contain a silent letter (see Related Words above). Have students identify the silent letter, and then suggest a mnemonic device to help them remember it. In some cases, simply pronouncing the word and exaggerating the silent letter can be a useful (not to mention humorous!) strategy.

2 Silent letters appear in some of the names of our fifty states, including Arkansas, Connecticut, and Illinois, as well as in the names of some nations, including Bhutan, Djibouti, Ghana, and Thailand. Have students locate such places on a map and mark the silent letters that could cause them spelling problems.

SOFT C, SOFT G

GOAL: To provide catalogs of words that have soft *c* and soft *g*, and to contrast the hard and soft sounds these two letters make

KEY CONCEPTS/RULES

• The letter *c* usually has a "hard" sound (/k/) when it precedes *a, o,* or *u* in a word.
• The letter *c* usually has a "hard" sound when another consonant follows it (*cloud, crow*).
• The letter *c* usually has a "soft" sound (/s/) when it precedes *e, i,* or *y* in a word.
EXCEPTIONS: *cello, special, ocean, racial, social*
• The letter *g* usually has a "hard" sound (/g/) when it precedes *a, o,* or *u* in a word.
• The letter *g* usually has a "hard" sound when another consonant follows it (*glass, great).*
• The letter *g* usually has a "soft" sound (/j/) when it precedes *e, i,* or *y* in a word.
EXCEPTIONS: *get, geese, give, girl*

RELATED WORDS

Initial	Medial	Initial	Medial
cease	acid	gee	danger
ceiling	bicycle	gelatin	energy
celebrate	concert	gem	engine
cell	dancer	Gemini	huge
cemetery	decision	gene	original
certain	fancy	generation	oxygen

ACTIVITY IDEAS

1 Prepare sets of index cards that contain a mix of soft *c* and hard *c* words, and other sets that present an assortment of soft *g* and hard *g* words. Invite pairs of students to sort the cards into piles of soft and hard sounds. For an additional challenge, include words that have both soft and hard letters in initial and medial positions.

2 Invite students to add words to a poster or interactive bulletin board that highlights soft and hard *c* and *g* sounds. Encourage them to include words they come across in their classroom reading and in discussions, or that appear in newspapers or magazines. Guide students to identify patterns in the examples they collect.

CONTRACTIONS

GOAL: To reinforce the role of the apostrophe in a contraction and to provide examples of commonly used contractions

KEY CONCEPTS/RULES

- A contraction is a word in which an apostrophe (') replaces one or more letters (*that's, can't, should've*).
- You can group most contractions by the word that is abbreviated: *am, are, is, has, would, had, have, will, not*.

RELATED WORDS

doesn't	isn't	mustn't	those'll
don't	it'd	she's	what's
here's	it'll	that'd	who've
I'm	let's	they'd	you're

ACTIVITY IDEAS

1 Reinforce the concept that all contractions have one or more letters taken away and replaced by an apostrophe. Use individual flannel letters on a flannel board, magnetic letter cards, or letter cubes to form pairs of words that could be made into common contractions. Prepare bright red apostrophes that students can substitute for the removed letter(s). Have students physically perform this action. Alternatively, present contractions with the apostrophe in the correct position and have students replace the apostrophe with the missing letter(s) for which it stands.

2 Many familiar titles of songs, plays, books, or films contain contractions. Examples include *You've Got Mail, She's the One, Can't Buy Me Love,* and *That's Entertainment*. Challenge students to find other examples of titles that include contractions. Extend by presenting well-known titles with the contracted words spelled out fully. Have students try to identify the familiar title.

TWO, TOO, or TO

GOAL: To provide mnemonics to help students determine which of these commonly used homophones to apply in written situations

KEY CONCEPTS/RULES

• The three words *two, too,* and *to* are known as homophones—words that sound alike but are spelled differently. Many people, including many well-educated adults, mix up these three words in written work. That's why words like these are often called "spelling demons"—they are frequently misspelled or misused.

• Homophones contain the same number of *phonemes* (units of speech sound), but different *graphemes* (written representations of phonemes).

• An effective way to learn *two, too,* and *to* is to develop some memory tricks, or mnemonic devices, that can help differentiate them. Here are some examples:
  • *Two,* the number, has a *w* in it, as in *how* many.
  • *Too* has too many *o*'s.
  • *Also* has two syllables—like the two *o*'s in *too.*
  • *To,* the preposition, goes by so fast, it's the shortest to spell.

RELATED WORDS

*two*fold	in*to*
two-piece	on*to*
*two*some	*to*-and-fro
two-by-four	*to*-do

ACTIVITY IDEAS

1 Compose paragraphs or sets of sentences with missing words represented by blank spaces. Have students fill in each blank with *two, too,* or *to,* based on context and usage. Example:
Liza decided _____ go _____ the mall for the _____ hours she had _____ fill until her dental appointment. _____ bad that her favorite shop was closed for inventory!
[*Answers: to; to; two; to; Too*]

2 Divide the class into three groups. Give each group one of the homophones *two, too,* or *to* written on an index card. Provide chart or poster paper. Have groups brainstorm for five minutes to list phrases that demonstrate the correct use of the given homophone. Then have groups switch homophones and repeat the activity until each group has worked on all three homophones. Display the posters and discuss what students have written.

SPELLING ACE
(Contemporary rock & roll)

CHORUS

    Spelling ace, spelling ace, spell long words at a blistering pace,
    Spelling ace, spelling ace, get those letters in their place!
    Spell 'em in rhythm, spell 'em in rhyme, spell 'em out just about anytime,
    Be a spelling ace!

Have you ever been accused of *exaggeration*?
Have you made something small seem bigger than it is?
It's a long, strong word to spell again and again,
E-X-A-G-G-E-R-A-T-I-O-N, exaggeration, E-X-A-G-G-E-R-A-T-I-O-N, exaggeration.
Once you've got it, you're a spelling ace!

See a play or hear a speech in the *auditorium*,
Be in the audience to clap or cheer,
It's a long, strong word to be overcome,
A-U-D-I-T-O-R-I-U-M, auditorium, A-U-D-I-T-O-R-I-U-M, auditorium.
Once you've got it, you're a spelling ace!

There's lots of facts and dates in the *encyclopedia*.
Charts and maps and details for any idea,
It's a long, strong word to practice every day,
E-N-C-Y-C-L-O-P-E-D-I-A, encyclopedia, E-N-C-Y-C-L-O-P-E-D-I-A, encyclopedia.
Once you've got it, you're a spelling ace!

CHORUS

Keep your groceries fresh in the *refrigerator*,
Eggs and milk and cheese, cold pizza for later,
It's a long, strong word for a cool gold star,
R-E-F-R-I-G-E-R-A-T-O-R, refrigerator, R-E-F-R-I-G-E-R-A-T-O-R, refrigerator.
Once you've got it, you're a spelling ace!

Miscellaneous means a bunch of this and that,
An assortment or variety of chit and chat.
It's a long, strong word to put you to the test,
M-I-S-C-E-L-L-A-N-E-O-U-S, miscellaneous, M-I-S-C-E-L-L-A-N-E-O-U-S, miscellaneous.
Once you've got it, you're a spelling ace!

Immediately means that you've got to handle it,
No time to waste, do it here and now!
It's a long, strong word that can hurry by,
I-M-M-E-D-I-A-T-E-L-Y, immediately, I-M-M-E-D-I-A-T-E-L-Y, immediately.
Once you've got it, you're a spelling ace!

CHORUS

WALTZING ENDINGS

(Viennese waltz)

CHORUS
  1-2-3, 1-2-3, waltzing and gliding,
  A-B-L-E? I-B-L-E? Which one is hiding?
  1-2-3, 1-2-3, waltzing along,
  A-B-L-E? I-B-L-E? Try it with song!

If it's out of your sight, it's *invisible*.
I-N-V-I-S, plus the end.
I-N-V-I-S plus I-B-L-E,
It's invisible, invisible — I-B-L-E.

If it easily bends, it's *flexible*.
F-L-E-X plus the end.
F-L-E-X plus I-B-L-E,
And it's flexible, flexible — I-B-L-E.

If it's likely to happen, it's *possible*.
P-O-S-S, plus the end.
P-O-S-S plus I-B-L-E,
Makes it possible, possible — I-B-L-E.

CHORUS

If you like it you call it *enjoyable*.
E-N-J-O-Y plus the end.
E-N-J-O-Y plus A-B-L-E,
It's enjoyable, enjoyable — A-B-L-E.

If it's broken I hope that it's *fixable*.
That's F-I-X plus the end.
F-I-X plus A-B-L-E,
And it's fixable, fixable — A-B-L-E.

It can go through the wash so it's *washable*.
W-A-S-H plus the end.
W-A-S-H plus A-B-L-E,
And it's washable, washable — A-B-L-E.

You can do it yourself when you're *capable*.
C-A-P, plus the end.
C-A-P plus …
Yes, you're capable, capable — A-B-L-E!

CHORUS

K-N

(Jug band tune)

CHORUS

    K-N sounds like *N* when it starts a syllable or word,
    K-N sounds like /n/, my friend, even though this seems absurd.
    K-N, K-N, didn't you **k-n**ow?
    Silent *K,* Granny told me so,
    K-N sounds like *N* when it starts a syllable or word.

Papa never **k-n**ew when guests might come 'round **k-n**ocking.
With their big old **k-n**uckles on our **k-n**otty pine front door.
Well, it's always un**k-n**own who might be home,
K-neeling on the cabin floor,
Papa never **k-n**ew who'd be **k-n**ocking anymore.

Sister got a **k-n**ot in the yarn she used for **k-n**itting,
She never got the **k-n**ack of untanglin' all her life.
Well, it's common **k-n**owledge, Granny **k-n**ows
When she's scrubbing the cabin floor,
Cut the fat old **k-n**ot with a big old carving **k-n**ife.

CHORUS

Brother **k-n**elt down for to empty his bulging **k-n**apsack,
There was so much in it that he surely didn't rightly **k-n**ow
Where he got the door**k-n**ob and the new **k-n**ick**k-n**acks
That he tossed upon the cabin floor,
His **k-n**apsack's a whole lot lighter now, you **k-n**ow!

Mamma met a **k-n**ave and a **k-n**ight on the road to **K-n**oxville,
They wore woolen **k-n**ickers for to hide their old **k-n**ock-**k-n**ees.
Mamma laughed herself silly as a **k-n**ockout punch
As she rolled on the cabin floor,
Cook the soup, **k-n**ead the bread, go slice the cheddar cheese.

CHORUS

K-nave, **k-n**ack, **k-n**elt, **k-n**ight, **k-n**ock, **k-n**ow, **k-n**ew!

SILENT *E*

(Calypso ballad)

CHORUS

    Silent *E*! Silent *E*!
    Powerfully changing words noiselessly.
    Silent *E*!

On a summer day with a gentle breeze
I'd like to fly a kite up over the trees,
Start with K-I-T, *kit,*
Then you'll see what happens when you add silent *E,*
It's *kite* — K-I-T-E, *kite.* Silent *E*! Silent *E*!

I wish upon a star twinkling in the sky,
I hope my wish comes true, by and by.
Start with H-O-P, *hop,*
Then you'll see what happens when you add silent *E,*
It's *hope* — H-O-P-E, *hope.* Silent *E*! Silent *E*!

We like to hear music every day,
So let's pop in a tape and let it play.
We like to hear music every day,
So let's pop in a tape and let it play.
Start with T-A-P, *tap,*
Then you'll see what happens when you add silent *E,*
It's *tape* — T-A-P-E, *tape.* Silent *E*! Silent *E*!

My soda's too warm, so it needs some ice.
Add a frosty cube, that's the best advice.
Start with C-U-B, *cub,*
Then you'll see what happens when you add silent *E,*
It's *cube* — C-U-B-E, *cube.* Silent *E*! Silent *E*!

turn the page

SILENT E

(continued)

I hurt my little foot, it's so hard to move,
I'll need to use a cane as I improve,
Start with C-A-N, *can*,
Then you'll see what happens when you add silent *E*,
It's *cane* — C-A-N-E, *cane*. Silent *E*! Silent *E*!

I want to see the whole wide world someday,
To travel the globe to places faraway.
I want to see the whole wide world someday,
To travel the globe to places faraway.
Start with G-L-O-B, *glob*,
Then you'll see what happens when you add silent *E*,
It's *globe* — G-L-O-B-E, *globe*.

CHORUS

DOUBLE TROUBLE
(Sea chantey)

Want to avoid the double trouble?
Want to avoid the double trouble?
Listen for the vowel and you won't flub,
You'll use a rule to spell well.

CHORUS
    Short vowels take a consonant double,
    Short vowels take a consonant double,
    Listen for the vowel and you won't flub,
    You'll use a rule to spell well.

Is it *dinner* or is it *diner*?
Is it *finner* or is it *finer*?
Listen for the vowel as a warning sign,
You'll use the rule to spell well.

Is it *hopping* or is it *hoping*?
Is it *lopping* or is it *loping*?
Listen for the vowel and stop your groping,
Use the rule to spell well.

CHORUS

Is it *tinny* or is it *tiny*?
Is it *whinny* or is it *whiny*?
Listen for the vowel so bright and shiny,
Use the rule to spell well.

Is it *scarred* or is it *scared*?
Is it *starred* or is it *stared*?
Listen for the vowel to be prepared to
Use the rule to spell well.

CHORUS

Interlude: Arrgghhh! Me *bonny* lass…
             Ach! You *bony* pirate!

Is it *tapping* or is it *taping*?
Is it *scrapping* or is it *scraping*?
Listen for the vowel and keep escaping,
Use the rule to spell well.

Is it *planned* or is it *planed*?
Is it *canned* or is it *caned*?
Listen for the vowel and you'll be trained to
Use the rule to spell well.

CHORUS

WHY CHANGE Y TO I?

(Cowboy & Western tune)

CHORUS

Ay-yi-yi-yi-yi, what to do about *Y*!

Yippee yi, yippee yo, yippee why change *Y* to *I*?

Why, old buddy, tell my why,

Why do you lose that final *Y*?

Why does it change from *Y* to *I*, my friend?

— To add some endings to the end!

— To add some endings to the end!

He got a *fancy* cowboy shirt about a week ago,

F-A-N-C-Y as a rodeo,

I got a *fancier* shirt for me,

Can you spell it now so we all agree?

F-A-N-C-I-E-R

Change that pesky *Y* to *I* — what for?

— To add the ending *E-R*!

She raised a *dandy* horse named Rosalie,

D-A-N-D-Y as a honeybee,

I've got the *dandiest* horse in town,

Can you spell it now before the sun goes down?

D-A-N-D-I-E-S-T

Change that pesky *Y* to *I* — you see!

— To add the ending *E-S-T*!

CHORUS

We're *lucky* to live out in the West,

L-U-C-K-Y as a treasure chest,

Life is fine here *luckily*,

Can you spell it now so we all agree?

L-U-C-K-I-L-Y

Change that pesky *Y* to *I* — you know why!

— To add the ending *L-Y*!

CHORUS

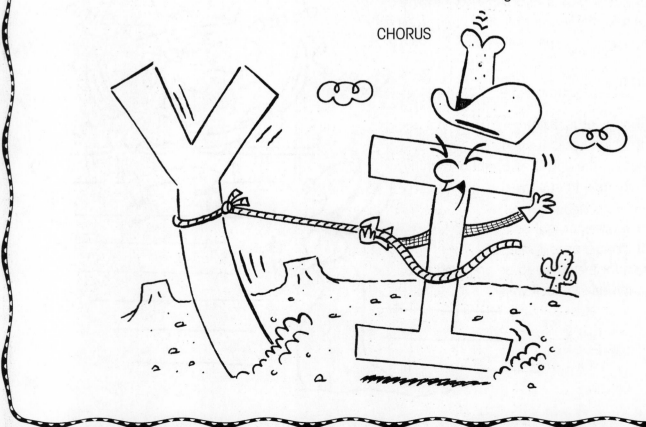

HOMOPHONES

(Pop/reggae)

CHORUS
    Homophones always sound the same,
    But their meanings are different, it's a crying shame.
    And they need different letters, nobody to blame.
    Which one is which in the homophone game?

Everybody's wanting *peace* on earth, P-E-A-C-E,
Feast on a *piece* of coconut pie, P-I-E-C-E,
What do you do if you're *bored* today, B-O-R-E-D?
Learn to do a flip off the diving *board*, B-O-A-R-D!

B-L-E-W, oh how those winter winds they *blew*!
B-L-U-E, oh how I love my *blue* suede boots!
T-H-R-O-U-G-H, tunneling *through* with you,
T-H-R-E-W, what a fastball the pitcher *threw*!

If it's more *than*, it's T-H-A-N whenever you compare,
Don't mix it up with T-H-E-N when it's *then* and there,
B-R-E-A-K, you say, when it's tiny little pieces that *break*,
Brake with B-R-A-K-E for the stop your bike must make!

CHORUS

Never you mind that crawly *ant*, that little-bitty A-N-T,
Brush it away, then hug *Aunt* Mae, A-U-N-T,
She was born long ago back in the *past*, P-A-S-T,
That's her old neighborhood that we just *passed*, P-A-S-S-E-D.

Come with me to S-A-I-L our *sail*boat over the sea,
We're heading for the S-A-L-E *sale* at the grocery!
We'll spend our money on a *berry* tart, that's B-E-R-R-Y,
Then we'll *bury* our dazzling treasure chest, B-U-R-Y.

Welcome to *our* town, it's O-U-R whenever it's yours and mine,
It sounds quite a bit like H-O-U-R, that's the *hour* when you're telling time,
S-C-E-N-E, a *scene* that has actors in a play,
S-E-E-N, I've *seen* it once or twice already today!

CHORUS

SNEAKY *O-U-G-H*

(Tango)

CHANT

    O-U-G-H, O-U-G-H, O-U-G-H

    /off/, /uff/, /oh/, /ow/, /aw/, /oo/.

I know a sneaky group of letters most spellers wish had never met,
Four letters that make six different sounds, don't you worry, don't you fret!
What are these devious letters that can confuse your ears and eyes?
O-U-G-H, O-U-G-H — now let's get wise.

The smoggy air can make you *cough*, that's C-O-U-G-H,
Those letters you hear, they tell your ear it's the /off/ sound, O-U-G-H.
Hear the /off/ in the cattle *trough* where the animals get their feed,
C-O-U-G-H, T-R-O-U-G-H, *cough*, *trough*.

You want to stop, you've had *enough*, that's E-N-O-U-G-H,
Those letters you hear, they tell your ear it's the /uff/ sound, O-U-G-H.
Hear the /uff/ if it's *rough* and *tough*, then you'll know which letters to use,
R-O-U-G-H, T-O-U-G-H, *enough*, *rough*, *tough*.

To make fresh bread you knead the *dough*, that's D-O-U-G-H,
Those letters you hear, they tell your ear it's the /oh/ sound, O-U-G-H.
Hear the /oh/ even *though* you have used those letters before,
D-O-U-G-H, T-H-O-U-G-H, *dough*, *though*.

CHANT

turn the page

SNEAKY *O-U-G-H*

(continued)

I spied an owl on the highest *bough*, that's B-O-U-G-H,
Those letters you hear, they tell your ear it's the /ow/ sound, O-U-G-H.
Hear the /ow/ on any *bough* and behind the farmer's *plough*,
B-O-U-G-H, P-L-O-U-G-H, *bough, plough*.

Add a T for a brand new *thought*, that's T-H-O-U-G-H-T,
Those letters you hear, they tell your ear it's the /aw/ sound, O-U-G-H-T.
Hear the /aw/ in what you *bought* or in what you *fought* so long,
B-O-U-G-H-T, F-O-U-G-H-T, *thought, bought, fought.*

One last sound to go on *through*, that's T-H-R-O-U-G-H,
Those letters you hear, they tell your ear it's the /oo/ sound, O-U-G-H.
Hear the /oo/ *through* and *through*, it's the only word like that,
T-H-R-O-U-G-H, T-H-R-O-U-G-H, we're *through*, we're *through.*

Now we know a sneaky group of letters most spellers wish had never met,
Four letters that make six different sounds, we won't worry, we won't fret
Because we know those devious letters that can confuse our ears and eyes,
O-U-G-H, O-U-G-H — we just got wise!

TRICKY SILENT LETTERS

(R & B rap)

CHORUS

    It's a trap! It's a trick!
    Some letters seem to get a kick
    Out of being where they don't seem to need to be
    To make spelling harder than it ought to be,
    To make spelling harder than it ought to be.

There's a tricky little *O* that goes inside all *people*,
P-E-O-P-L-E, *people*, yes indeed!
Once you're certain that you know that you need that tricky *O*,
You'll spell it right each time,
P-E-O-P-L-E, *people*, you so-and-so!

Don't forget that skinny *L* that lurks in every *half*,
It's H-A-L-F, *half*, now what a laugh!
Once you know you need an *L*, it's easier to spell, and
You'll spell it right each time,
H-A-L-F, *half*, fare thee well!

CHORUS

Who wants a whopping *W* inside *answer*?
It's A-N-S-W-E-R when it's right.
Once you add the *W*, you'll know what to do,
You'll spell it right each time,
A-N-S-W-E-R, *answer*, that's the clue!

Did it occur to you that you need a *U* in *tongue*?
It's T-O-N-G-U-E, I learned today.
Once you know you need a *U*, there's no stopping you,
You'll spell it right each time,
T-O-N-G-U-E, *tongue*, koo-koo-ka-joo!

CHORUS

It's hard to believe that you need a *B* in *doubt*,
It's D-O-U-B-T, *doubt*, and that's no lie.
Once you remember the *B*, you can smile with glee,
You'll spell it right each time,
D-O-U-B-T, *doubt*, unquestionably!

No matter how hard you try and try to *listen*,
It's L-I-S-T-E-N, *listen* with a tiny *T*,
Once you know you need the *T*, it's as easy as can be,
You'll spell it right each time,
L-I-S-T-E-N, *listen*, tweedle-dee-dee!

CHORUS (repeat 2 times)

SOFT *C*, SOFT *G*

(Rhythmic lullaby)

Softly, so softly, how soft *C* can speak,
Peacefully … and totally unique,
Hard *C* is **c**olorful, it's **c**risp and it's **c**lear,
But soft *C* has sparkle, it's /sss/ to the ear.

Citrus, **c**ider, **c**innamon, and **c**ent,
Celery, **c**entury, **c**yberspa**ce**, **c**ement,
Cereal, **c**inema, **c**itizen, pre**c**ise,
Census, **c**ylinder, **c**eramics, and i**ce**.

Softly, so softly, how soft *C* can speak,
Peacefully … and totally unique,
Hard *C* is colorful, it's **c**risp and it's **c**lear,
But soft *C* has sparkle, it's /sss/ to the ear.

Gently, so gently, how soft *G* can change,
Generous, but **g**iant and stran**g**e,
Hard *G* is **g**alloping, it's **g**allant and **g**ray,
But soft *G* is gentle, it sounds like a *J*.

Gingerbread, **g**entlemen, **g**ypsy, **g**eolo**g**y,
Genuine, **g**eranium, **g**iraffe, **g**eometry,
General, **g**erbil, **g**emstone, and **g**ender,
Geor**g**ia, **g**ibberish, **g**enius, **g**esture.

Gently, so gently, how soft *G* can change,
Generous, but **g**iant and strange,
Hard *G* is **g**alloping, it's **g**allant and **g**ray,
But soft *G* is gentle, it sounds like a *J*.

Softly, so softly, how soft *C* can speak,
Peacefully … and totally unique,
Hard *C* is **c**olorful, it's **c**risp and it's **c**lear,
But soft *C* has sparkle, it's /sss/ to the ear.

But soft *G* is gentle, it sounds like a *J*.
But soft *C* has sparkle, it's /sss/ to the ear.

CONTRACTIONS

(Oldies-style bluesy rock)

To form a contraction requires subtraction,
You take away a letter or more.
To form a contraction requires action,
You know what we're looking for?
To spell a contraction, it's a chain reaction—
A mark like a comma in the air,
Apostrophe!

Who is the captain of the soccer team?
Why champ, that's right—*you are*!
Y-O-U and A-R-E, no kidding, oh yes, *you are.*
But why spell two words separately
When you can let one letter simply go scot-free,
Then link what's left with an apostrophe:
Y-O-U ' R-E!

Can you lift an elephant over your head?
Why, partner, that's right, you *cannot*.
C-A-N and N-O-T, you *cannot,* we both agree.
But why spell two words separately
When you can let two letters simply go scot-free,
Then link what's left with an apostrophe:
C-A-N ' T!

turn the pag

CONTRACTIONS

(continued)

So here's a useful tip to help you know if you need an apostrophe:
Do you have two words that can link as one if a letter or two go free?
Look for a place where you'd have a gap,
Then jump right in with a contraction trap.
Now don't you get it, isn't it a snap?
Apostrophe!

Which of us is gonna take the cake?
Why, brother, that's right, *we will.*
W-E and W-I-L-L, *we will,* oh can't you tell!
But why spell two words separately
When you can let two letters simply go scot-free,
Then link what's left with an apostrophe:
W-E ' L-L!

Who may have spilled the chocolate milk?
Why, buddy, that's right, we *could have.*
C-O-U-L-D and H-A-V-E, we could have spilled it easily.
But why spell two words separately
When you can let two letters simply go scot-free,
And link what's left with that apostrophe:
C-O-U-L-D ' V-E!

To form a contraction requires subtraction,
You take away a letter or more.
To form a contraction requires action,
You know what we're looking for?
To spell a contraction, it's a chain reaction—
A mark like a comma in the air,
Apostrophe!

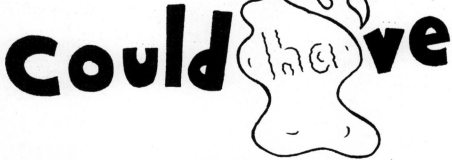

TWO, TOO, or TO

(Ragtime)

CHORUS

    Toot-toot-tootledy-too, now where's the clue?
    Toot-toot-tootledy-too, when it could be *two, too,* or *to*?
    Know which *TO* you need to write
    So you'll absolutely, positively get it right,
    Know your *two* from your *too* from your *to*,
    That's what to do!

Let's begin with the number *two,* you know that it's T-W-O,
You need three letters for the number *two,*
What a silly-nilly way to go!
6, 5, 4, 3, 2 — T-W-O, it's the number *two,*
Toot-tootle-loo and tootledy-too
T-W-O, now count to *two*!

CHORUS

Now when you mean to say "also," then it's T-O-O
Two *o*'s in a row if you mean "also," it's *too,* that's T-O-O!
(When it's *too* darn hot, you need those *o*'s a lot!)
T-O-O, it's so *too too,*
Toot-tootle-loo and tootledy-too
T-O-O, you kangaroo!

So every other *to* that you need to do is just little ol' T-O,
To the moon, *to* prefer, *to* him or *to* her,
It's T-O, little T-O.
T-O, *to* come or *to* go,
T-O, *to* shrink or *to* grow,
T-O, eeny-meeny-miney-mo!
Toot-toot-tootledy-too and toot-toot-tootledy-too!

CHORUS